Drug Testing in Schools

A Pro/Con Issue

Jennifer Lawler

Enslow Publishers, Inc.

40 Industrial Road	PO Box 38
Box 398	Aldershot
Berkeley Heights, NJ 07922	Hants GU12 6BP
USA	UK

http://www.enslow.com

Library of Congress Cataloging-in-Publication Data

Lawler, Jennifer, 1965–
    Drug testing in schools : a pro/con issue / Jennifer Lawler.
      p. cm. — (Hot pro/con issues)
    Includes bibliographical references and index
    Summary: Presents arguments on both sides of the controversial
question of whether schools should test students for drug use, and
provides a history of drug testing.
     ISBN 0-7660-1367-7
     1. Students—Drug testing—United States—Juvenile literature.
  [1. Drug testing.] I. Title. II. Series.
  HV5823.5.U6 L38 2000
  371.7'84'0973 21–dc21

                                                99-041165

Printed in the United States of America

10 9 8 7 6 5 4 3 2 1

To Our Readers:
All Internet addresses in this book were active and appropriate when we
went to press. Any comments or suggestions can be sent by e-mail to
Comments@enslow.com or to the address on the back cover.

Contents

Chapter 1

The Debate Over Drug Testing

Matthew, a football player, was looking forward to playing in Saturday's game. He was scheduled to start at linebacker, a position he played well. The opposing team was top-rated and a tough rival. Matt was nervous because drug testing had shown that two players on his team had been using creatine. (Creatine is a nutritional supplement used by some athletes to build up their muscles.) The two were suspended from the team for taking a banned substance. Without these two players, the offensive line was going to have a tough time.

The coach told everyone that some nutritional supplements were banned for football players at his school. The coach said creatine is like steroids and since steroids are dangerous, the school had to ban it. To make sure everyone followed the rules, the athletic department routinely tested student-athletes for drug use.

A few days before the game, Matt came down with a cold. He started taking an over-the-counter cold medicine so that he could get through practice without suffering too much. Just before the game, he was tested for drugs, according to school policy. Then the coach told Matt that the cold medicine he had been taking had ephedrine in it. Ephedrine is a stimulant that the school had banned. Matt's coach had no choice but to suspend him.

Matt heard many people complain about his suspension—friends, family, and fans. They all wanted to know why a football player could not even take a cold medicine. They wondered what gave the school the right to suspend athletes for taking legal drugs. They also wondered why Matt was tested for drug use in the first place. He had never even been suspected of using illegal drugs. No one really understood, and Matt had a hard time explaining it himself. For a long time, drug testing had made sense to him. It was used to stop athletes

School Activities and Drug Use

(for grades 6-12)
39.4% of students who NEVER participate in school activities use drugs
36.1% of students who SELDOM participate in school activities use drugs
26.8% of students who SOMETIMES participate in school activities use drugs
23.6% of students who OFTEN participate in school activities use drugs
20.5% of students who participate in school activities A LOT use drugs

Source: *12th Annual PRIDE National Survey of Student Drug Use (1998-1999)*, Office of National Drug Control Strategy, Bureau of Justice Statistics Sourcebook, September 8, 1999.

*M*any coaches warn young athletes about taking certain nutritional supplements that contain steroids. Here, Chicago Bears quarterback Jim Miller talks about his four-game suspension. Miller had taken a nutritional supplement not knowing that it contained an anabolic steroid.

from taking dangerous drugs. It was also to stop them from using drugs that could artificially improve performance. Considering his suspension, Matt was not so sure now that drug testing made sense.

Drug testing in the workplace and at school is designed to help detect and prevent drug abuse. Along with illegal drugs, other drugs may be banned by schools for a variety of reasons. For example, students may be banned from using alcohol and nicotine, since most students are under the legal age to purchase and use these drugs. Students who are athletes may be prohibited from using performance-enhancing drugs, such as steroids, since these are considered dangerous. These drugs may also give students who take them an unfair advantage over students who do not. In order to tell if students are using any of these drugs, schools sometimes use drug testing.

Supporters of drug testing in schools say that by identifying drug users, drug-related problems can be prevented and drug abusers can be helped to recover. They say that drug use should not be tolerated in students. They believe that drug testing is a safe and accurate method for identifying drug users. But other people doubt that drug testing reduces drug use. They say drug users simply switch to drugs that are not tested for or use different methods to fool drug tests. Also, critics of drug testing in schools say that even if drug testing does what it is supposed to do, it violates too many rights, such as the right to privacy.

By reading what each side has to say about this issue, one can make up his or her mind. A person can decide whether to support or oppose drug testing in schools.

Chapter 2

The History of Drug Testing

Throughout history, drugs have been used for medical, recreational, and religious reasons. Not all drugs are bad or must be avoided. Medicinal drugs are helpful, even life-saving, such as when a doctor prescribes medication to treat high blood pressure. This is called therapeutic drug use. But drug misuse or abuse harms people. Drug misuse happens when a person uses a drug in a way it was not meant to be used. Drug abuse happens when a person feels he or she must have a certain drug no matter what. Because even some therapeutic drugs can be misused and abused, the government has made many rules about buying and using drugs.[1]

Why Drug Use Can Be Dangerous

Drugs that can be bought in a store without a prescription are called over-the-counter medications. These include cough syrups, mild pain relievers, and cold medicines. Although these medications can have side effects such as drowsiness,

Types of Drugs

The Controlled Substances Act was created in 1970 by the United States government to help in its fight against drug abuse. The act places all drugs into one of five groups, or schedules. A drug's placement is based on its medical use, safety, and potential for abuse or dependence.

Schedule I

✓The drug has a high potential for abuse.

✓The drug has no currently accepted medical use in the United States.

✓There is a lack of accepted safety for use of the drug under medical supervision.

✓Some Schedule I substances are heroin, LSD, and marijuana.

Schedule II

✓The drug has a high potential for abuse.

✓The drug has a currently accepted medical use in treatment in the United States or a currently accepted medical use with severe restrictions.

✓Abuse of the drug may lead to severe psychological or physical dependence.

✓Schedule II substances include morphine, PCP, cocaine, and methamphetamine.

Schedule III

✓The drug has less potential for abuse than the drugs in Schedules I and II.

✓The drug has a currently accepted medical use in treatment in the United States.

✓Abuse of the drug may lead to moderate or low physical dependence or high psychological dependence.

✓Anabolic steroids, aspirin or Tylenol containing codeine, and some barbiturates are Schedule III substances.

Schedule IV

✓The drug has a low potential for abuse relative to the drugs in Schedule III.

✓The drug has a currently accepted medical use in treatment in the United States.

✓Abuse of the drug may lead to limited physical dependence or psychological dependence relative to the drugs in Schedule III.

✓Included in Schedule IV are Darvon, Talwin, Equanil, Valium, and Xanax.

Schedule V

✓The drug has a low potential for abuse relative to the drugs in Schedule IV.

✓The drug has a currently accepted medical use in treatment in the United States.

✓Abuse of the drug may lead to limited physical dependence or psychological dependence relative to the drugs in Schedule IV.

✓Over-the-counter cough medicines with codeine are classified in Schedule V.

Source: "Controlling Drugs or Other Substances," United States Department of Justice. n.d., <http://www.usdoj.gov/dea/concern/abuse/chap1/contents.htm> (December 15, 1999).

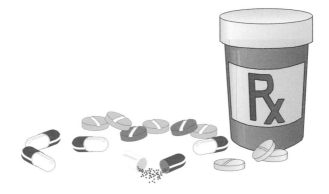

they are considered safe drugs. However, it is possible to abuse over-the-counter medications, take an overdose, or even die from them.

Some drugs, like alcohol and nicotine, are legal for adults to use. Although legal, these drugs can cause problems like disease and dependency. Some prescription medicines can also be misused or abused. For example, anabolic steroids are used to treat certain diseases. However, some athletes misuse them to increase their strength and body weight. Misuse of steroids is dangerous. It can cause liver damage, high blood pressure, and aggressive behavior. Some drugs have little medical value and can be very dangerous. These are completely illegal.

Rules about buying and using drugs exist because drug abuse causes many problems. The main problem is that people sometimes come to depend on drugs. They let drug use interfere with and even ruin their lives. A person who thinks he or she needs a certain drug has psychological dependency. A person whose body relies on the drug and who has physical symptoms if drug use is stopped has physical dependency. Such physical symptoms are called withdrawal symptoms. They include shaking, sleeplessness, tension, seizures, hallucinations, and even death. Drug tolerance means the user needs more and more of a drug to get the same effect.[2]

Drug addiction, sometimes called drug dependency, occurs when a person can no longer control his or her use of a drug. He or she continues to use a drug even after bad consequences. Drug addicts may stop caring about themselves, their families, and their friends. They stop trying to do well in school or at work. They may find it impossible to stop using drugs.

Studies show that in the United States, more than half a million deaths each year are directly caused by tobacco, alcohol, and other drug use. Use of these drugs costs taxpayers and employers more than $215 billion each year. This figure includes law enforcement efforts, medical costs, days absent from work, and other economic losses.[3]

A drug education organization called PRIDE took a survey of students to learn about their drug habits. The survey showed that more than 4 million students, age eleven to eighteen, use illegal drugs regularly.[4] This fact, along with the dangers of drug abuse, has caused considerable concern among parents, lawmakers, teachers, and others.

Origins of Drug Testing

Drug testing first began in treatment centers to keep tabs on addicts and their recovery. In the late 1970s and early 1980s, amateur and professional sports organizations began testing athletes for drug use. Their main concern was performance-enhancing drugs, which could give one athlete a competitive advantage over another. Even the slightest edge can make the difference between winning and losing in competitive sports. In addition, using illegal drugs, such as marijuana and cocaine, can be dangerous. In pro sports, such drug use can cost team owners a lot of money. If an athlete does not play at his or her best or is arrested or injured while using drugs, the team owner can lose millions of dollars. Most athletic unions have agreed to limited drug testing programs for their athletes.

The Federal Government and Drug Testing

Around the same time that sports organizations began testing athletes for drugs, the military started drug testing. Soon, the federal government began testing workers in certain jobs for drug use. At first, only workers directly involved in public safety and security were tested. Next, the courts decided that transportation workers such as truck drivers who used drugs were a "clear and present" danger to the country. For this reason, transportation workers could be forced to take drug tests even if there was no reason to suspect they were using drugs.

In the 1980s, the federal government began investing millions of dollars in a program called the War on Drugs. Drug testing became part of this war.

*T*he United States military routinely tests soldiers for drug use.

The government felt that the only way to reduce the demand for drugs, especially among casual users, was to identify users. Drug users could then be offered counseling or could be punished for using illegal drugs. The easiest way to do large-scale drug testing was to ask employers to test employees for illegal drug use.

In 1986, President Reagan issued an executive order saying that certain federal agencies had to test employees for drugs. These were agencies most concerned with public health and safety. Other agencies were required to test for drugs when there was reasonable cause or suspicion of drug use, as part of an investigation into an accident, or in connection with rehabilitation for addicts.

The Drug-Free Workplace Act of 1988 required businesses and institutions receiving federal funds to ensure that their employees were drug free. Most businesses attempted to meet this requirement by drug testing.[5] Public Law 102-240 (1991) requires companies with commercial drivers of trucks and other motor vehicles to have strict rules against substance abuse and to do drug testing.

Drug Testing in Schools

Once workplace drug testing became common, school officials began to think that drug testing in schools could help prevent many problems. After all, if drug use and abuse affect the ability of adults to work, it would certainly affect the ability of students to succeed.

Most people think that testing for drugs is okay when a student appears to be under the influence. However, not everyone agrees that drug testing should be used when a student does not appear to be using drugs—that is, drug testing without cause. Although many Americans support drug testing in the workplace and at school, many others oppose it. This has led to a debate about whether drug testing is necessary or even legal.

It has not been as easy for public schools to force students to undergo drug testing as it has been for employers to force workers to undergo drug testing. The main reason is that private organizations such as most businesses and private schools can require potential employees or students to meet whatever standards they want, within certain limits. Although private organizations cannot discriminate based on race, they can say that all their employees must pass drug tests. A person who does not want to be tested for drugs could find a job somewhere else.

On the other hand, public organizations, such as public schools, are more limited in the conditions they can impose. The reason is that a person is considered to have a basic right—as well as an obligation—to attend school. If a person attending public school is required to take a drug test as a condition of attending school, then the student's right to privacy and his or her right to be free from illegal search and seizure have been violated. Unlike private organizations, public schools cannot force students to undergo drug testing without cause, according to legal analysts—and the U.S. Supreme Court.[6]

For this reason, the focus of drug testing in schools centers on students involved in extra-curricular activities such as sports. Since students do not have to take part in these activities, testing participants for drug use has been considered legal by a number of courts. In October 1998, the U.S.

The Fourth Amendment

Some people think that drug testing in schools violates a student's right to be free from illegal search and seizure. This right is outlined in the Fourth Amendment to the Constitution, which reads:

The right of the people to be secure in their persons, houses, papers, and effects, against unreasonable searches and seizures, shall not be violated, and no warrants shall issue but upon probable cause, supported by oath or affirmation, and particularly describing the place to be searched, and the persons or things to be seized.

Supreme Court upheld these rulings in the court case *William R. Todd and Diana Todd* v. *Rush County Schools.*[7]

Drug-Testing Terms

Even though drug testing of students involved in extracurricular activities may be legal, the debate continues. In the drug-testing debate, words like mandatory, voluntary, arbitrary, and random are used. What do these words mean? Mandatory drug testing means that people are forced to undergo testing. If a person refuses, he or she could be fired, suspended from school, or sent to jail. Voluntary drug testing means that a person agrees to undergo a drug test. For example, a person agrees to be tested to prove that he or she was not impaired at the time of an accident. Arbitrary drug testing means that person is tested for drug use even if he or she does not appear to be using drugs. Random drug testing means that people are selected by chance to undergo drug testing, even if no one suspects them of drug use. For example, all of the high school football players might have their names put in a box and the first three people whose names are pulled out of the box must undergo drug testing. The element of chance ensures that everyone has an equal likelihood of being selected.

Types of Drug Testing

Testing for drugs is done in different ways. Blood, hair, urine, breath, and even sweat can be used for testing. The sample is treated with chemicals to determine if specific drugs have been used. Coordination tests such as attempting to walk a straight line can also show evidence of drug use. Observation is another test. Watery, red eyes can sometimes be a sign of drug use. Drooping eyelids, a blank stare, and jerky eye movements are also signs of impairment. Coordination and observation tests do not indicate the type of drug being used, but they can be accurate indicators of drug use. Observation and testing for coordination are not as invasive as other types of drug tests.[8]

A Breathalyzer, which is a device that measures the amount of alcohol on a person's breath, is often used by police officers during traffic stops. The person is asked to breathe into a tube and the device tests for alcohol use. Breathalyzers are used by some schools to test for alcohol use before dances and even during the school day. The results of a

Breathalyzer test are considered accurate evidence of alcohol use.

Other Drug Tests

Some drug tests can be done without the subject knowing it. These drug tests can tell whether a person has been carrying drugs. However, they cannot determine if the person has actually been using the drugs. A machine called IONSCAN works like metal detectors in airports to detect whether a person is carrying illegal drugs. It is now used in England and France as a nonintrusive way to

*T*he IONSCAN machine can tell if a person is carrying illegal drugs. It is similar to a metal detector (pictured) which determines whether a person is carrying weapons.

determine if travelers possess illegal drugs. It is also used in the United States at some prison facilities.[9]

Another product, called Drug Alert, is a chemically treated cloth that picks up traces of drugs on furniture, books, or any object in the environment. It is marketed to parents who want to know if their children are using drugs. The company that promotes the product assumes that if a child possesses or has handled drugs, he or she is probably using them.

Some schools install metal detectors to prevent students from bringing guns to school. Perhaps schools will one day install IONSCAN to prevent students from bringing drugs, and wipe down lockers with Drug Alert cloth to see if they contain drugs. As testing grows more sophisticated and less obvious, it is likely to be used more often in the workplace, home, and school.

Commonly Used Drug Tests

But most drug tests require more cooperation from the person being tested. Most tests measure a person's drug use through the laboratory analysis of urine, hair, or blood.

The most common drug test is urinalysis. A urine sample is sent to a lab, which uses chemical tests to determine if certain drugs are present. People who want to beat these tests sometimes try to use masking agents to hide drug use. Some companies even sell powdered urine that people undergoing drug testing can use in place of their own urine. To prevent these things from happening, people being tested for drug use are sometimes required to provide the sample in the presence of a witness,

Effectiveness of Urinalysis

Drug Tested	Effectiveness
Alcohol	Not very effective; test must occur within hours of use.
Marijuana	Very effective, up to three or four weeks after use.
Cigarettes	Effective up to forty-eight hours after use.
Smokeless Tobacco	Effective up to forty-eight hours after use.
Cocaine	Effective up to forty-eight hours after use.
LSD	Unable to detect.
Steroids	Very rarely tested due to high cost of tests.
Inhalants	Not tested.
Heroin	Effective up to seventy-two hours after use.
Other Opiate Narcotics	Effective up to seventy-two hours after use.
Amphetamines	Effective up to seventy-two hours after use.
Barbiturates	Very effective up to one to two weeks after use of the drug.
Tranquilizers	Effective up to three to five days after use.

Source: *Indiana Prevention Resource Center at Indiana University,* "Alcohol, Tobacco and Other Drug Use Survey," 1998, <http://www.indiana.edu/resources/indiana.html> (March 1, 2000).

such as a nurse or a lab employee. This can be embarrassing for the person taking the drug test.

Hair testing is sometimes used, since it is less embarrassing and less invasive than urine testing. A portion of a person's hair is cut off as closely to the scalp as possible. The hair is then given several different chemical tests. Hair testing has other advantages over urine testing. Traces of drug use usually leave the body quickly, so a urine test may be negative even though a person has used drugs recently. However, evidence of drug use can show up in the hair weeks and even months after use. Another advantage of testing hair is that a hair test cannot be fooled the same way a urine test can. Some people have used bleach, hair color, and other such agents in an attempt to destroy evidence of drug use, but these efforts have proven unsuccessful.

Blood tests, which require blood samples to be drawn, are never used in schools. However, in some amateur and professional sports, blood testing may be used in certain circumstances. It is hard to tamper with blood samples.

Accuracy of Drug Tests

Of the different methods of drug testing, blood tests are usually the most reliable, followed by urine tests and then hair tests. Hair tests have been accused of being racially unfair. A component of African-American hair makes it as much as fifty times more likely to test positive for drug use than Caucasian hair. Brunette hair is more likely to test positive for secondhand smoke, so if a brunette person is even around a person smoking marijuana, he or she may test positive for drug use. Blonde Caucasians, then, are least likely to test positive with this method, regardless of actual drug use.[10] "There is overwhelming evidence that there is color bias in hair testing," says Dr. Bruce Goldberger, a researcher at the University of Florida.[11] Further, hair testing has not been proven to be scientifically accurate. "It's potentially possible that people could have detectable levels [of a drug] in their hair without ever using the drug," says Michael Welch, a scientist with the National Institute of Standards and Technology.[12]

Urine testing, frequently used in school drug-testing programs, can be over 90 percent accurate when conducted according to National Collegiate Athletic Association (NCAA) standards. But only two laboratories in the country have achieved certification by the NCAA.[13] Since school districts cannot usually afford to spend two hundred dollars or more to have each sample tested at such a laboratory, they rely on cheaper, less accurate tests. Sometimes they do not do a second test to double-check positive samples, since these "double-check" tests are more sophisticated and expensive. Inexpensive, quick tests may be simple to administer, but they can be less than 50 percent accurate.[14]

Questions About Drug Testing

Although most people find drug testing acceptable if there is evidence of drug use, not everyone agrees that random drug testing is acceptable. Because random testing affects everyone, it is important to understand why people believe it should—or should not—be done.

Whether or not students use drugs, drug testing

concerns them. Is drug testing justified? Should it be routine? Mandatory? Who should be tested? What should be done to those who test positive?

One reason there is so much debate over drug testing is that it pits two sets of very important rights against each other. One set includes the rights of individuals—the right to privacy, the right to fair treatment under the law (due process), and the right to be protected from unreasonable search and seizure. The other set includes the rights of the public—the right to be protected from potentially dangerous drug users, the right to prevent costly social and economic problems that stem from drug use, and the right to live and learn in a healthy, safe environment.

Chapter 3

Why Students Should Be Tested

Although drug use among adults has declined by about 50 percent since the mid-1980s, the number of teens using drugs has in some cases doubled or even tripled since 1991, according to 1998 statistics.[1]

Several studies suggest that teens are less aware of the risks of drug use now than in the past. A 1998 survey taken by the Partnership for a Drug-Free America (PDFA), a drug education organization, showed that most teens do not see a great risk in trying certain drugs. For example, 46 percent of teenagers believe methamphetamine is a low-risk drug. This belief is common even though meth-amphetamine is a highly addictive, dangerous drug. More than three quarters of surveyed students do not see any danger in trying marijuana. Since teens do not have a true understanding of the risks they take when they try drugs, some people argue, adults have the responsibility to detect their drug use in order to treat it.

Role of Parents

Should school administrators, not parents, be the ones to decide if young adults should be tested? Supporters of school drug testing say that even those parents with the best intentions are not always able to effectively educate their children about the dangers of drug use. The PDFA survey showed that almost 80 percent of parents believe their children understand the risks of drug use. However, as many as 80 percent of teens do not think there is much risk in trying certain drugs. Parents overestimate how much teens know about drug use. They mistakenly believe that their children understand the risks.

At the same time, more than 30 percent of the teens surveyed said their parents never talked to

| Drug Use When Parents Talk About Drugs ||
Parents' Role	Grades 6 through 12
Parents Never Talk About Drugs	**35.0%** of students use drugs
Parents Seldom Talk About Drugs	**29.3%** of students use drugs
Parents Sometimes Talk About Drugs	**23.9%** of students use drugs
Parents Often Talk About Drugs	**23.3%** of students use drugs
Parents Talk A Lot About Drugs	**21.9%** of students use drugs

Source: *12th Annual PRIDE National Survey of Student Drug Use (1998–1999)*, Office of National Drug Control Strategy, Bureau of Justice Statistics Sourcebook, September 8, 1999.

them about drugs. Only 25 percent of teens said their parents had talked to them about drugs in the past year.[3] This is true even though most young adults say they would like their parents to talk more about drugs.

Parents also underestimate "the reality of drugs in their own children's lives," according to the PDFA survey. "Parents . . . recognize the severity of the drug problem but few sincerely believe their children are exposed to drugs, that drugs are widely available in school," the survey concludes.[4] For example, only about 20 percent of parents say they believe their children have tried marijuana. However, almost half of all teens admit to having tried it. More than one third of all teens were offered drugs in school in 1997 by other students. Many parents do not recognize the dangers their children face. Therefore, supporters of drug testing say schools have a responsibility to control student drug use. They feel that drug testing is one solution.

Role of Schools

Supporters of drug testing in schools argue that students are under the protection of the school when they are there. Just as locker searches without permission or cause have been deemed acceptable, they say, drug testing should also be acceptable. After all, schools do have the responsibility to control and supervise students in a way that would not be necessary or desirable for adults. Schools should use any means necessary to prevent and stop drug use, including drug testing. Supporters say drug testing in schools does not interfere with the role of parents, but instead reinforces it.

*S*ome schools test for alcohol use before events such as dances. The high school in Grant, Nebraska, requires students, faculty, and chaperones to pass a Breathalyzer test before allowing entry to the prom.

could even persuade casual users to stop. In one Ohio school district, students say that drug testing has discouraged marijuana use.[7]

Help Students Resist Peer Pressure

Finally, supporters say drug testing in schools helps students resist peer pressure. Highland, Ohio, school superintendent Michael Carson says, "If students were at a party and if there were drugs being passed around and they did not want to take them under normal circumstances, there would be peer pressure." But, he says, "if they could say, 'I can't do that because I'll be tested,' it gives them an excuse to say no."[8]

Although drug testing can be embarrassing and intrusive, supporters say, in the long run it stops students from ruining their lives and the lives of others.

Random Testing of Select Student Groups

However, school districts have found that randomly testing all of their students for drugs is impractical. Not only is it extremely expensive, but it encourages lawsuits against the schools. In general, courts have upheld the right for school administrators to test students.

Instead of testing the entire student body, now tend to focus on particular groups of In some schools, any student involved in urricular activity can be forced to submit to ing. Why do schools single out certain gro say that not all students need to be teste usually choose student-athletes for drug t

Student Athletes

Why are s letes different from the general student pop ion? Some supporters of drug testing think athletes are at greater risk for injury and violence because of drug use. If they play while high, they might not realize they have been hurt or they may have less control over themselves.

Student-athletes also have coaches and others who might pressure them to use drugs to enhance performance. These are pressures that students

Risk Perception

"There is great risk in . . ."

Drug	% of tenth graders agreeing:
. . . *trying* heroin *once or twice without using a needle*	73.7%
. . . *smoking one or more packs of* cigarettes *a day*	62.7%
. . . *trying* crack *once or twice*	57.8%
. . . *trying* cocaine *once or twice*	51.6%
. . . *taking* LSD *once or twice*	45%
. . . *using* smokeless tobacco *regularly*	44.2%
. . . *trying* marijuana *once or twice*	19.2%
. . . *trying one or two drinks of an* alcoholic beverage	10.5%

Source: Monitoring the Future Study, 1999, <http://www.monitoringthefuture.org/data/99data.html> (January 28, 2000).

who do not participate in organized sports do not have to worry about.

In addition, supporters of drug testing say that many athletic role models use drugs. With role models such as these influencing them, student-athletes might be more likely to use drugs.

But the most important reason schools test certain groups rather than all students is that the courts and the law allow them to. In 1995, the U.S. Supreme Court decided in *Vernonia School District* v. *Wayne Acton* that schools have a right to test athletes for drugs, and, by extension, any student who participates in an optional extracurricular activity.[9] The Acton lawsuit was brought by James Acton and his parents when James was a seventh-grade basketball player. His parents objected when school officials required a drug test of all students who wanted to play basketball. There was no evidence that James himself had used drugs. The Actons believed that mandatory drug testing without suspicion of drug use was unconstitutional. The Supreme Court disagreed. In the decision, Justice Antonin Scalia wrote, "The state's power over schoolchildren . . . permit[s] a degree of supervision and control that could not be exercised over free adults."[10]

Since this court decision, more and more schools are testing athletes for drug use. However, there is little evidence that athletes use more drugs than nonathletes. Many studies show little or no difference between drug use by athletes and nonathletes. Other studies indicate that athletes use more alcohol, smokeless tobacco, and steroids than non athlete students, but they use fewer cigarettes and less marijuana and cocaine.[11] Athletes are more

*S*upporters of drug testing believe that student-athletes are at a greater risk for injury and violence from drug use than other students are.

likely to engage in high-risk behavior, such as drinking and driving, but this is not the subject of drug tests. Also, athletes were more likely to use drugs out of season rather than during their sport's season. This may be because they do not want drug use to interfere with their sports performance. It may also be because they are afraid of being tested for drugs during the season. Supporters of drug testing say this shows drug testing deters drug use. They argue that if drug testing were done in the off-season as well, use of drugs among student-athletes would decline even further.

Reasons Why Student-Athletes Use Drugs

Amateur sports organizations routinely test student-athletes for drugs. The National Collegiate Athletic Association (NCAA), for example, requires college athletes to be tested for about eighty banned substances. Why hold athletes to higher standards than nonathletes? Because drugs are often used in sports to improve performance. Nonathletes do not take drugs for this reason. Some performance-enhancing drugs, like caffeine or aspirin, are legal and acceptable by sports organizations. Anabolic steroids, which some athletes use to build up their muscles, are legitimately used for medical conditions such as osteoporosis (bone loss) and certain kinds of cancer. But using anabolic steroids to build muscle can be dangerous. Also, it gives the athlete an unfair advantage in competition. Testing for it—and other performance-enhancing drugs—protects the student's health and ensures good sportsmanship. Student-athletes are also tested for illegal drug use, since this jeopardizes their health and lives.

Supporters of drug testing for student-athletes point out that athletes are especially vulnerable to using drugs to cope with stress. They receive a lot of attention, both good and bad. They expect a lot from themselves, have many demands on their time, and can be isolated from family and friends because of their busy schedules. They must be aggressive on the field, but under control off it. These tensions can contribute to an athlete's tendency to use drugs.

Pressure to perform better or to recover from an injury faster can cause an athlete to misuse drugs. Painkillers mask pain. Steroids build muscle.

Drug Use of Different Groups Compared to the General Student Body				
Drug	**Use by High School Athletes**	**Use by Middle School Athletes**	**Use by High School Extra-curricular Participants**	**Use by Middle School Extra-curricular Participants**
Alcohol	**10%** more likely to use*	**20%** less likely to use	**10%** less likely to use	**20%** less likely to use
Marijuana	**20%** less likely to use	**30%** less likely to use	**20%** less likely to use	**30%** less likely to use
Cigarettes	**20%** less likely to use	**30%** less likely to use	**10%** less likely to use	**10%** less likely to use
Smokeless Tobacco	**20%** more likely to use	**20%** more likely to use	**10%** less likely to use	**10%** less likely to use
Cocaine	**20%** less likely to use	**20%** less likely to use	**20%** less likely to use	**20%** less likely to use
LSD	**20%** less likely to use	**30%** less likely to use	**30%** less likely to use	**30%** less likely to use
Steroids	**20%** more likely to use	**10%** more likely to use	**10%** less likely to use	**10%** less likely to use
Inhalants	**10%** less likely to use	**10%** less likely to use	**10%** less likely to use	**10%** less likely to use
Heroin	**40%** less likely to use	**40%** less likely to use	**20%** less likely to use	**20%** less likely to use
Other Opiate Narcotics	**20%** less likely to use	**20%** less likely to use	**10%** less likely to use	**10%** less likely to use
Ampheta-mines	**10%** less likely to use	**10%** less likely to use	**10%** less likely to use	**10%** less likely to use
Barbitu-rates	**10%** less likely to use	**10%** less likely to use	**10%** less likely to use	**10%** less likely to use
Tranquil-izers	**10%** less likely to use	**10%** less likely to use	**10%** less likely to use	**10%** less likely to use

*All percentages are compared to the general student body.

Source: "Alcohol, Tobacco and Other Drug Use" Survey, Indiana Prevention Resource Center, 1998.

Amphetamines cause weight loss. All of these types of drugs are used, misused, and abused by some athletes for these reasons.

Also, supporters of drug testing argue, drug use makes athletes more likely to fix games, gamble, or otherwise engage in illegal or unethical acts to support their drug habits. This is a costly problem even in amateur athletics.

For the most part, the courts agree that student athletes can be subject to random, mandatory drug testing. The courts say that extracurricular activities are a privilege, not a right. No one is compelled to join a sports team. Courts have also ruled that schools can have higher expectations for such students, even including their behavior off-campus, since they serve as role models for other students.[12] For these reasons, many schools now randomly test student-athletes for drug use.

Expanding School Drug Testing

Some school districts, such as Dade County in Florida, have instituted voluntary drug testing for all students, in which parents give permission for their children to be tested for drugs. Results of these tests are supposed to be given only to the parents. If a student's drug test is positive, a report is sent to the student's parents, describing what drugs were found and where parents can go for help.

Some would like testing to become mandatory for all students. Dade County school board member Sandy Ojeda says, "The kids in trouble are not the ones whose parents would give consent. The parents are not part of their lives. That's why they are in trouble."[13] Many politicians agree. Former Speaker of the House Newt Gingrich has called for mandatory drug testing of all students. "We need to test kids," he says, "and that should be a condition of going to school."[14]

That does not seem likely for now. However, more and more school districts are choosing to test athletes for drug use. Many school districts are also beginning to test students involved in any extracurricular activity, such as drama or choir. Others require students who drive to school or who attend school dances to be checked for drug use, including alcohol. They feel the benefit gained from testing these students for drugs outweighs any harm it may cause.

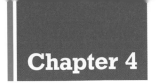

Chapter 4

Why Students Should Not Be Tested

The American Academy of Pediatrics strongly opposes drug testing of children and young adults. The organization believes that drug testing is not the solution to the drug problem and that involuntary testing is not right. "Students and student-athletes should not be singled out for involuntary screening for drugs of abuse. Such testing should not be a condition for participation in sports or any school functions," the organization states.[1]

Drug Testing Does Not Work

Supporters of drug testing often use statistics to show how drug use declines after drug testing is started. Critics say these statistics have little basis in scientific research. Many studies contain flaws in how they were carried out. They also produce results that could be interpreted in different ways. Critics of drug testing say that no scientifically valid study shows that drug testing decreases drug use.

Critics point out that drug-testing companies, who make huge profits on drug tests, conduct much drug-testing research. Therefore, drug companies have an interest in "proving" that drug testing works. They also contribute large sums of money to political campaigns so that politicians will support drug testing.[2]

Critics say that drug testing does not reduce the demand for drugs. Users simply switch from one drug to another. Some drugs, like LSD, are hard to detect through drug tests. This can even create more problems. Users can switch to a more dangerous drug if they are afraid of testing positive for something less dangerous, such as marijuana.

Drug Use Has Increased Since Drug Testing Began

Critics of drug testing also point out that drug use is now rising among young people. This has happened since the introduction of drug testing. Some analysts attribute this to a decline in drug education. Schools should educate students about risks rather than test them for no reason, opponents of drug testing believe. Schools should be used for education, not for monitoring students and enforcing drug laws, critics say.[3] Instead of testing for drugs, schools should set a positive example. Rules against drug use should be clear, opponents of drug testing say. Counseling for those with drug problems should be provided. Instead, too many schools focus on punishing students who use drugs, rather than on offering education about drugs and treatment assistance.

Drug Availability	
"It would be fairly easy or very easy to get this drug."	
Drug	**% of tenth graders agreeing:**
Marijuana	78.2%
Amphetamines	41.3%
Cocaine	36.7%
Crack	36.5%
Steroids	35.9%
LSD	34.3%
Barbiturates	33.2%
Narcotics (Besides Heroin)	26.6%
PCP	24.5%
Heroin	23.7%
Crystal Meth	21.8%
Source: Monitoring the Future Study, 1999, <http://www.monitoringthefuture.org/data/99data.html> (January 28, 2000).	

Drug Testing Violates Constitutional Rights

Critics point out that mandatory drug testing involves collecting evidence against people who are not even suspected of a crime. A drug test requires the innocent to prove their innocence, which violates the Constitution's guarantee of "innocent until proven guilty." Such drug testing invades a person's privacy and is a form of illegal search and seizure. The Fourth Amendment to the U.S. Constitution protects citizens from unreasonable search and seizure—that is, search and seizure carried out with no evidence of wrongdoing. Because students are sometimes watched while urinating to prevent cheating, their privacy is violated. They have every reason to feel humiliated and upset.[4]

Illegal Search and Seizure. The Fourth Amendment allows some searches without probable cause, when the invasion of privacy is minimal and the need for protection great. An example is the use of metal detectors at airports. The inconvenience to passengers is minor, and the protection from terrorists is high. Supporters of drug testing say drug testing is similar. The violation of an individual's rights is minor compared to the protection drug testing offers society. But critics disagree. Collecting urine from someone not suspected of a crime is much more invasive and embarrassing than asking someone to walk, fully clothed, through a metal detector.

Right to Privacy. Some supporters of drug testing claim the drug problem overrides privacy. Only the guilty have something to hide, so everyone else should accept drug testing. But critics say violating constitutional rights is never acceptable. Besides, drug testing does not just reveal whether or not a person uses illegal drugs. It can also reveal more about a person's health than is necessary for school officials to know. This makes a person's private concerns public. For instance, a urinalysis can reveal pregnancy and many other conditions. Drug tests may reveal that a student is taking medication for depression or another illness that school officials do not need to know about.

Right to Due Process. Drug testing also violates a citizen's right to due process, critics say. Due process means that legal actions must be carried out according to established rules. It guarantees basic fairness in legal proceedings. Testing someone for drug use for no better reason than because he or she is a student or student-athlete violates the meaning of due process. If a drug test is positive, the student usually has no way to appeal. The results of the drug test may be wrong, but that does not matter. The student can be kicked off the team, suspended from school, or otherwise punished without having a chance to defend himself or herself. School records follow students to every school they attend, which may have an impact on how they are treated.[5]

Right to Remain Silent. Critics also say that drug testing violates the Fifth Amendment. This amendment guarantees that "no one shall be compelled in any criminal case to be a witness against himself." This is popularly called "the right to remain silent." Forcing a person to provide a urine sample that turns out to test positive for drugs is a way of making a person be a witness against himself or herself. For this reason, critics of drug testing say, it is clearly illegal.

Drug Testing Creates a Negative Environment

Drug testing can also create negative and hostile feelings. Students who find themselves considered guilty until proven innocent have every reason to feel angry about it. Drug testing can create anger and can even work against prevention. For drug testing to work effectively, students must believe they could be tested at any time. Such attempts to make students fearful have no place in a school setting, critics say.[6] Further, drug testing implies that students cannot be trusted to remain drug-free. If no evidence of drug use exists, and drug tests are still used, students may feel resentful and rebellious. This may cause drug testing to backfire.

Mixed Messages

Critics say that drug testing sends mixed messages. Evidence shows that alcohol is the most widely misused drug among all school-aged children but it is rarely tested for. Nicotine, which is also illegal for minors, is at least as dangerous as some other banned substances, but it is not tested for either. The message is that alcohol and nicotine, even though they are illegal for minors to purchase, are all right to use. Some tests, such as steroid tests, are so expensive that few schools use them. Thus, student-athletes quickly learn that they can use some drugs without getting caught.

Another mixed message is that some drugs that allow an unfair advantage are accepted while others are not. For example, football players are not allowed the unfair advantage of taking steroids, but they can take novocaine or another strong painkiller to help them play better if injured.

And when only athletes are tested, it may send the message that the health of athletes matters more than the health of other students. Or it may send the message that athletes are more likely to use drugs than other students.

Inaccurate Tests

Critics of drug testing also say that supporters overlook how many drug-test results are inaccurate. Although drug-testing equipment becomes more precise each year, many errors still occur. Mistakes can be made during sample collection, labeling, storage, transportation, during the test itself, and when reporting on findings. According to the American Civil Liberties Union, between 10 and 20 percent of all drug-test results are false positives.

This means someone tests positive for an illegal drug he or she has not used.[7]

Even the most accurate drug screens must have backup tests run on positive samples, but few school districts are willing to pay for second, more expensive tests.

The quality of drug testing varies widely, as does skill in testing. Only eighty-five of twelve thousand labs in the United States have passed federal certification requirements. However, schools are not required to use certified labs. When labs are tested for accuracy in controlled studies (they do not know they are being tested), they are accurate only 46.5 percent of the time.[8]

In addition to showing false positives, drug tests can be inaccurate in other ways. For example, tranquilizers show up for very short periods of time. However, marijuana can show up for months after use, long after the drug has had any effect on the student. It can possibly show up long after the student has stopped using the drug entirely. Hallucinogens, such as LSD, rarely show up on tests.

Some diseases, like diabetes, cause certain chemicals to be produced in the body that can give false positives for cocaine, opium, and barbiturates. A student with a disease can be wrongfully accused and punished for drug use. In addition, passive contact, such as being near marijuana smokers at a concert, can lead to a false positive.

Legitimate foods and legal drugs may also throw off drug-test results. Ginseng tea and ibuprofen (pain reliever) can show up as marijuana. Poppy seed, used in many cakes and breads, can show up as heroin. Legally prescribed barbiturates, used to treat seizure disorder, anxiety,

*C*ritics of drug testing say that testing for only a few banned substances but not for nicotine, which is also illegal for teens, sends a mixed message. Nicotine is found in tobacco, which is used in cigarettes.

and insomnia, show up as illegal drugs. Over-the-counter medicine such as cold remedies can contain ephedrine, which shows up as an amphetamine. Even if a student submits a list of legal medications he or she uses, labs and school officials do not always compare test results with these lists. Besides, being forced to give out private medical information such as the medication one uses violates a student's right to privacy. Furthermore, what is to prevent a student from claiming he or she took cold medicine if he or she is afraid that amphetamine use will show up on the drug test? What purpose does drug testing serve if a positive test result can be explained away like this? Critics say these questions cancel out any usefulness of drug testing.

*S*ometimes, drug tests give a false positive result. Harmless substances, such as herbal tea, can show up as marijuana in a drug test.

A false positive drug test could seriously damage a student's academic life, personal life, reputation, and future. Even an accurate positive test can be unfair. One positive test does not mean that a student is addicted to a drug, just as a negative drug test does not guarantee that a student is drug-free.[9]

Drug-test results end up in student records. Inaccurate tests can result in a student undergoing costly and unnecessary counseling. Drug-testing information, although supposedly confidential, is

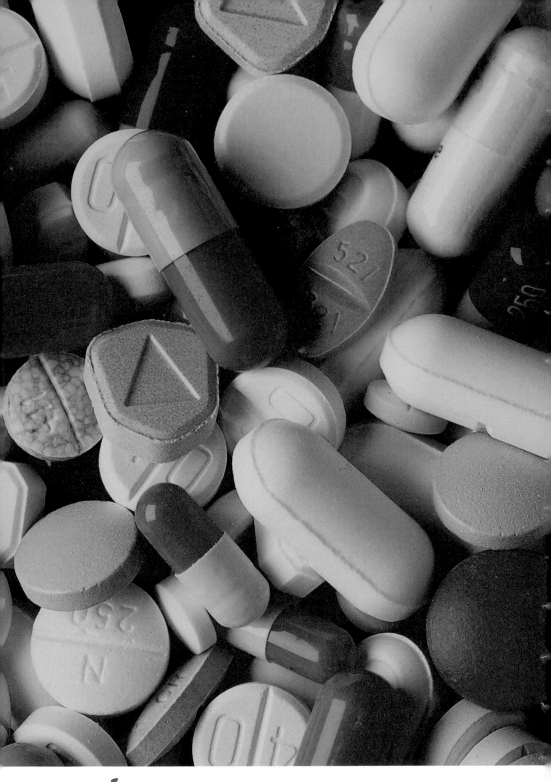

If a person takes an over-the-counter cold medicine that contains ephedrine, it may show up as the illegal drug methamphetamine on a drug test.

rarely treated as such. Everyone from the school secretary to the homeroom teacher to the football coach could learn the results of a drug test without legally being entitled to know.[10] This would clearly affect how a student is treated in school and on the playing field.

Users Switch Drugs

Critics say that students often know which drugs are difficult to detect. They will use drugs that are eliminated from the system more quickly, such as cocaine. For example, a student could use marijuana on the weekend and then be tested at school some days later. The effects would have worn off, but the student could still be punished for drug use. On the other hand, a student could snort cocaine before class on Monday and it would not show up on a drug test until later that day. Although the student would be high and possibly a danger to himself or herself and others, a drug test would be negative.

The Fort Worth, Texas, school district, for example, started a drug-testing program that tested for only five drugs: marijuana, PCP, cocaine, opiates, and amphetamines. Users, knowing this, could simply switch to a drug not tested for.[11]

Students Beat Drug Tests

In addition, many drug users know how to beat drug tests. This means the people most likely to be caught are the innocent, the first-time users, and the casual users—the people least likely to have a drug problem. Entire businesses exist to help people beat drug tests. People can purchase drug-free powdered urine or take confidential tests to make sure their urine is clean. On-line, teens have easy access to information on beating drug tests.[12]

Student-athletes may also try to beat the tests by stopping drug use before scheduled tests. For example, they may stop taking steroids six weeks before competition or they may take steroids only in the off-season. This makes drug testing useless and encourages deceit, critics say.

Students may also try to beat a drug test in potentially dangerous ways such as taking large doses of vitamin C to eliminate evidence of drug use or taking antacids or unneeded antibiotics to mask cocaine, sedatives, and amphetamines.[13]

Expense of Drug Testing

Critics also point out that drug tests cost more than schools can really afford to spend. Some cheap urine tests cost one hundred dollars. Some do-it-yourself tests cost even less, but they are all very unreliable. Unreliable tests have an extremely high social and personal cost. But the real economic cost is not how much each individual test costs. Since the purpose of using drug testing is to discover who is using drugs, the amount that matters is how much it costs to obtain an accurate positive result. If no one tests positive, and drug users falsely test as drug-free, there is not much point in drug testing.

One government study showed that less than 1 percent of more than thirty thousand workers tested positive. Almost $12 million was spent on testing. Therefore, each positive test cost $77,000. In one Chicago school district, student-athletes were randomly tested for alcohol and ten other drugs. Two hundred seventy-seven players were tested at the rate of fifteen per week. This cost $50,000 at a time when the district could not even afford new playing equipment.[14]

In 1998, Miami schools were criticized for spending hundreds of thousands of dollars on a random drug-testing program that did not offer follow-up treatment. The only action school officials planned was to tell parents if their children failed. Students would not be tested without parental permission, and would not be punished for opting out. What, exactly, was the point? critics asked. If parents wanted to know if their children used drugs, they could ask them. Parents could also invest in an inexpensive home drug test or ask the family doctor to perform a drug test to get an accurate answer. Critics say there are better uses for school resources, including drug education and treatment programs.

Critics also point out that one of the dangers of drug testing is overreliance on it as a tool for detecting drug use. Instead, teachers and parents should look for signs of drug use, such as lower grades, new friends, or a change in personality.

Drug Testing Leads to Punishment, Not Prevention

Critics also say that drug testing may lead to students being punished. Students who test positive are kicked off the team or out of school. Testing leads to punishment, not prevention or rehabilitation. And even if drug testing did lead to earlier treatment, critics point out that people are not forced to undergo other medical procedures such as blood tests or x-rays unless there is a reason to suspect that a person has a disease.[15] Why do we force them to undergo drug tests if we do not suspect them of drug use?

In the past few years, several school districts have stopped student drug testing because of these concerns. At the same time, many more schools are considering starting drug-testing programs. But opponents of drug testing say that drug abuse is a complex problem. Drug testing, which appears to be a simple solution, is not a solution at all. Critics say that part of living in a free society means putting up with some undesirable consequences of freedom, such as drug use. They say solving complicated problems requires complex solutions, and drug testing is not one of them.

Chapter 5

Conclusion

Supporters of drug testing say that drug tests can discourage students from using drugs, make parents aware of drug use, and help students get the assistance they need. However, mandatory random testing of all students in a school is still rare. This is because public schools are government institutions and must obey the guidelines of the Constitution, particularly the Fourth Amendment. Some school districts that have tried drug-testing programs have found them ineffective and expensive.

But drug testing of student-athletes, effective or not, appears to be here to stay. These programs are popular among the general population. They are used by amateur and professional sports organizations. Nonetheless, the question still remains: Should drug testing be allowed in schools? And if so, who should be tested?

Supporters of drug testing say that testing can help prevent many problems associated with drug use. It can help students get the treatment they need for drug problems. They say that parents cannot do a good enough job of detecting and treating drug use in their children, and that schools have a responsibility to protect young adults. They believe drug testing helps teach students about the dangers of drug use, counteracts pro-drug messages, and allows the early detection of drug use. Drug testing, they say, can also prevent drug-abuse problems by discouraging drug use and helping students resist peer pressure.

Opponents of drug testing say that testing results in punishment, not treatment. They argue that drug testing violates too many personal rights to be worth any benefit that might be gained. Critics say that drug testing does not reduce drug use the way

*L*indsay Earls (left) and Daniel James, both sixteen, have brought a lawsuit against their Tecemshe, Oklahoma, school because of its policy that requires drug testing for participation in some extracurricular activities and classes.

supporters believe it does. They believe that it is best to teach students about the dangers of drug use, and to provide treatment for those students who do have drug-abuse problems. Opponents believe drug testing leads to a negative school environment and mixed messages. Inaccurate tests can still have a big impact on a student's life. Students who use drugs may attempt to mask drug use to avoid detection. These methods can be dangerous and even deadly.

Al-Anon (for families of alcoholics)
Family Group Headquarters
1600 Corporate Landing Parkway
Virginia Beach, VA 23454-5617
(800) 344-2666
<http://www.al-anon-alateen.org>

Alcohol Hotline
(800) ALCOHOL, or (800) 252-6465

American Civil Liberties Union
125 Broad Street
New York, NY 10004-2400
(212) 549-2500
<http://www.aclu.org/>

Cocaine Anonymous
World Service Office
P.O. Box 2000
Los Angeles, CA 90049-8000
(800) 347-8998
<http://www.ca.org>

Cocaine Hotline
(800) COCAINE, or (800) 262-2463

Community Anti-Drug Coalitions of America
901 North Pitt Street, Suite 300
Alexandria, VA 22314
(703) 706-0560
(800) 542-5322
<http://www.cadca.org>

Drug Help
(800) DRUG-HELP, or (800) 378-4435
(information and referral)

National Clearinghouse for Alcohol and Drug Information
(800) 729-6686
<http://www.health.org>

National Council on Alcoholism and Drug Dependence, Inc. (NCADD)
12 West 21st Street
New York, NY 10010
(800) 622-2255
<http://www.ncadd.org>

National Drug Strategy Network
c/o Criminal Justice Policy Foundation
1225 Eye Street, NW, Suite 500
Washington, DC 20005
(202) 312-2015
Fax: (202) 842-2620
<http://www.ndsn.org>

National Steroid Research Center and Other Drugs of Abuse in Sports
(800) STEROID, or (800) 783-7643

Partnership for a Drug-Free America
405 Lexington Avenue, 16th Floor
New York, NY 10174
(212) 922-1560
<www.drugfreeamerica.org>

Resource Center on Substance Abuse Prevention
1819 L Street, Suite 300
Washington, DC 20036
(202) 628-8080

United States Olympic Committee Hotline Regarding Banned Substances
(800) 233-0393

Youth Crisis Hotline
(800) 448-4663

Chapter 1. The Debate Over Drug Testing

1. "Around College Football: Southeast," Associated Press, *CNNSI.com*, October 16, 1998, p. 2.

Chapter 2. The History of Drug Testing

1. "Drug Use in the General U.S. population," *1997 National Household Survey on Drug Abuse*, Substance Abuse and Mental Health Services Administration, U.S. Department of Health and Human Services. Fact sheet (1997).

2. David E. Larson, M.D., ed., *Mayo Clinic Family Health Book* (New York: William Morrow and Company, 1990), pp. 433, 439.

3. Joseph B. Treaster, "Police in New York Shift Drug Battle Away from Streets," *The New York Times*, July 28, 1992, p. A1.

4. *12th Annual PRIDE National Survey of Student Drug Use (1998-1999)*, Office of National Drug Control Strategy, Bureau of Justice Sourcebook, September 8, 1999.

5. Kent Holtorf, M.D., *Ur-ine Trouble* (Scottsdale, Ariz.: Vandalay Press, 1998), p. 23.

6. William Bailey, M.P.H., C.P.P., "Suspicionless Drug Testing in Schools," Indiana Prevention Resource Center, Indiana University, July 19, 1997, pp. 1–2.

7. United States Supreme Court Decision, no. 97-2548. *William P. Todd and Diane Todd* v. *Rush County Schools and Ed Lyskowsinski, Superintendent.* October 5, 1998.

8. Bailey, p. 3.

9. Ivan Penn, "Drug Testing System Screens Prison Workers in Maryland," *Baltimore Sun*, October 10, 1997, vol. 117, no. 49, p. A3.

10. Holtorf, p. 103.

11. "Color Bias in Hair Testing," *New York Daily News*, June 27, 1999, Substance Abuse News Summary Service.

12. "Drug Debate Intensifies Over Hair Testing Students," *The New York Times*, June 14, 1999. Substance Abuse News Summary Service.

13. Bailey, p. 3.

14. Holtorf, p. 69.

Chapter 3. Why Students Should Be Tested

1. "The Air War on Drugs," *The Washington Times*, January 13, 1998, report in Partnership for a Drug-free America Fact Sheet, June 1998, p. 16.

2. "Most Teens Don't See Great Risk in Methamphetamine," Partnership for a Drug-Free America, Press Release, June 17, 1998, pp. 1–2.

3. "Survey Finds Parents Unaware of Drug Use," *The Washington Post*, April 13, 1998, Op-Ed.

4. "Bulletin," Partnership for a Drug-Free America, Fact Sheet, June 1998, p. 1.

5. "The Monitor's View: Heroin Isn't Chic," *The Christian Science Monitor*, May 26, 1997, Op-Ed.

6. "Drugs in Cyberspace," *The News*, Newsletter of the Partnership for a Drug-Free America, vol. 11, no. 1, Spring 1998, p. 7.

7. "Drug Testing Working in Ohio Schools," *Akron Beacon Journal*, May 9, 1999, Substance Abuse News Summary Service.

8. "Ohio School District Approves Drug Testing," *Akron Beacon Journal*, November 18, 1998, Substance Abuse News Summary Service.

9. United States Supreme Court Decision, no. 94–590, *Vernonia School District 47J, Petitioner* v. *Wayne Acton*, et ux., June 26, 1995.

10. David G. Savage, "High Court Oks Routine Testing of Students for Drugs," *The Los Angeles Times*, June 27, 1995, p. A1.

11. Kevin R. Ringhofer, Ph.D, and Martha E. Harding, *Coach's Guide to Drugs and Sport* (Champaign, Ill.: Human Kinetics, 1996), p. 8.

12. Ibid., p. 38.

13. "Dade Parents Like School Drug Tests," *The New York Times*, September 28, 1997, Substance Abuse News Summary Service.

14. "Mandatory Drug Testing For Students," *Associated Press*, June 7, 1998.

Chapter 4. Why Students Should Not Be Tested

1. R. B. Heyman, et al., "Testing for Drugs of Abuse in Children and Adolescents," *Pediatrics*, vol. 98, no. 2, 1996, pp. 305–307.

2. Kent Holtorf, M.D., *Ur-ine Trouble* (Scottsdale, Ariz.: Vandalay Press, 1998), p. 9.

3. Kevin R. Ringhofer, Ph.D, and Martha E. Harding, *Coach's Guide to Drugs and Sport* (Champaign, Ill.: Human Kinetics, 1996), p. 4.

4. "ACLU Sues School District Over Drug Testing," *The New York Times*, August 18, 1999, Substance Abuse News Summary Service.

5. "Dole Calls for School Drug Testing," Associated Press, September 22, 1999. Substance Abuse News Summary Service.

6. William Bailey, M.P.H., C.P.P., "Suspicionless Drug Testing in Schools," Indiana Prevention Resource Center, Indiana University, July 19, 1997, p. 5.

7. Holtorf, p. 59.

8. Ibid., p. 69.

9. Ringhofer and Harding, p. 51.

10. Holtorf, p. 52.

11. "Parents, Students Condemn School Drug Testing," *Fort Worth Star-Telegram*, May 27, 1998, Substance Abuse News Summary Service.

12. "Drugs On Line: Cyberspace Information Should Concern Parents," *The Dallas Morning News*, July 24, 1997, Op-Ed.

13. Holtorf, pp. 112–117.

14. Ringhofer and Harding, pp. 141–147.

15. Holtorf, p. 32.

addict—A person who needs to use a drug.

addiction—The need to use a drug even after bad results or consequences.

alcohol—A depressant that can impair perception, motor skills, and judgment.

amphetamine—An addictive stimulant that increases performance, suppresses hunger, and decreases fatigue.

Bill of Rights—Constitutional document guaranteeing the rights of United States citizens and protecting them from government interference. The first ten amendments to the Constitution, which were accepted in 1791, are called the Bill of Rights.

caffeine—A mild stimulant found in chocolate, coffee, and some soft drinks.

casual user—A person who uses drugs recreationally but only occasionally; not an addict.

depressants—Drugs that relax the body and reduce body functions.

drug abuse—Using drugs, especially illegal drugs, in a harmful way, with loss of control over the drug use.

drug misuse—Using a drug for a reason other than its intended use.

due process—Guarantee of fairness in legal actions.

Fifth Amendment—Part of the Bill of Rights, it guarantees that no citizen will be "deprived of life, liberty or property without due process of law." It also guarantees that people do not have to testify against themselves in criminal cases.

Fourteenth Amendment—An addition to the Constitution, ratified in 1868, it extends the concept of due process to apply to the actions of state governments.

Fourth Amendment—Part of the Bill of Rights, it protects citizens from arbitrary or unreasonable search and seizure.

hard drugs—Illegal drugs that are considered to be the most dangerous and addictive, such as cocaine and heroin.

heroin—A narcotic that is usually injected into a vein. More recently, users have begun sniffing it to avoid using needles.

LSD (Lysergic Acid Diethylamide)—A hallucinogen that can cause anxiety, exhilaration, confusion, even psychosis (loss of contact with reality).

marijuana—A drug that is smoked, producing a sense of happiness and relaxation.

methamphetamine—A stimulant that is created in underground laboratories from common chemicals.

narcotics—Drugs that relieve pain, cause numbness, and induce sleep.

opium—A narcotic made from the poppy plant, which causes numbness and drowsiness.

PCP (phencyclidine)—A hallucinogen that can cause feelings of exhilaration, anxiety, and even psychosis (loss of contact with reality).

physical dependency—A condition that occurs when the body relies on a drug and will have physical symptoms if the drug is no longer used.

psychological dependency—A condition that occurs when a person thinks he or she needs the drug to feel better and to get along.

sedative—A drug used to relax the body and reduce body functions.

soft drugs—Illegal drugs that seem less dangerous and addictive than others. Marijuana is an example of a soft drug.

stimulants—Drugs that are used to excite or energize the body.

tobacco—A product whose main chemical, nicotine, is a stimulant. Tobacco use can cause numerous health problems, including cancer.

tolerance—The need to use more of a drug to get the same effect.

U.S. Constitution—Written document defining the rights of United States citizens and the federal government.

withdrawal—Physical symptoms that occur when a person stops using a drug. Also used to describe the psychological effects addicts suffer when they quit using a drug that causes psychological dependency.

zero tolerance—A policy under which the possession, use, or sale of any controlled substance is prosecuted, regardless of the amount of drug, the type of drug involved, or other circumstances.

Black, David L., ed. *Drug Testing in Sports*. Las Vegas: Preston Publishing Company, 1996.

Clayton, Lawrence. *Drugs, Drug Testing and You*. New York: Rosen Publishing Group, 1997.

Kuhn, Cynthia, Ph.D. *Buzzed*. New York: W.W. Norton & Company, 1998.

Ligocki, Kenneth. *Drug Testing: What We All Need to Know*. Bellingham, Wash.: Scarborough Publishing, 1996.

Nelson, Elizabeth Ann. *Coping With Drugs and Sports*. New York: Rosen Publishing Group, 1995.

Newton, David E. *Drug Testing: An Issue for School, Sports, and Work*. Springfield, N.J.: Enslow Publishers, Inc., 1999.

Peck, Rodney. *Drugs and Sports*. New York: Rosen Publishing Group, 1997.

Further Reading